Written by Catherine de Sairigné
Illustrated by Pierre Denieuil

*Specialist adviser: Steve Pollock,
The British Museum
(Natural History)*

*ISBN 1 85103 022 0
First published 1987 in the United Kingdom by
Moonlight Publishing Ltd,
131 Kensington Church Street, London W8*

*© 1985 by Editions Gallimard
Translated by Sarah Matthews
English text © 1987 by Moonlight Publishing Ltd
Printed in Italy by La Editoriale Libraria*

POCKET • WORLDS

Wild Life
in
Towns

Up and down the city streets,
inside and outside the houses...

THE ANIMAL WORLD

Look around you!

Sparrows are twittering on your windowsill. A grey mouse runs along the pavement, moths flutter around the street lamps... In towns, from attic to sewer, from garden to rooftop, all sorts of wild animals make their homes, despite all the concrete and the tarmac. A lot of them keep hidden, or only come out at night, and you don't glimpse them. Some, like the birds, are very familiar.

You will never see this termite. It never comes out.

Pigeons coo on the rooftops in the early morning.

A wasps' nest tucked under the eaves

In town, even the climate is different!

The animals don't get so cold in the winter, thanks to the warm houses and the heat from cars. High buildings block off the wind and provide ready-made shelter: this **lacewing** keeps safe there in winter. Spring arrives sooner in towns, the chestnut trees always have their leaves out earlier! Nights are not so dark under the street-lamps... And there is so much food about: dustbins, greengrocers' stalls, flower-beds provide good things to eat all year round!

Blue-tits love to peck through bottle-tops to drink the delicious cream at the top of your pint of milk.

Spiders are our friends.

They eat all sorts of insects!

The commonest spider you see in your home is the **house spider.** It spins its web in corners to catch its prey. When the victim is caught, the spider carries it off to eat. All that is left is the husk!

This **harvestman** catches prey with its immensely long legs. If it's attacked, it will leave a leg behind in order to get away.

Spiders change skins as they grow. You can sometimes find the empty skins.

House fly   Bluebottle   Greenbottle

The creepy-crawly empire of insects

Insects are the most numerous inhabitants of a town. And they're the ones that do us most harm! What attracts flies to our kitchens? Leftovers, cheese, meat... They settle on food left uncovered and lay their eggs. The eggs hatch out into maggots which soon grow into flies...

Not all mosquitoes bite.

Only the female needs our blood, before she lays her eggs on stagnant water.

Mosquitoes squirt saliva into the bite to stop the blood clotting. That's what makes it itchy!

Before they turn into moths, the grubs of the clothes moth eat holes in curtains, clothes and carpets.

Who is that eating my house?
Termites and **wood-worms** eat wood. They can chew a whole roof-frame into sawdust. When wood-worm emerge, they leave little round holes. Termites never come out, they don't like the light. Nothing stops them: if they come up against concrete, they just go round it!

Earwigs look fierce with their big pincers, but they don't hurt you. They live in the cracks between the floorboards, and come out at night to feed.

Female earwigs lay their eggs in the soil, and look after them carefully.

Silverfish!

Woodlice like dark, damp places.

It's a lovely name for a shy little scaly insect. There have been silverfish on Earth for over 350 million years. You can sometimes see them at night when they come out to find a few crumbs to eat.

Human flea

Head louse

Silverfish like eating glue and paper

Insects that suck our blood

<u>Fleas</u> can live for several months without eating. They can jump as much as 30 centimetres high: a huge height for such a tiny animal!

A cockroach. The female lays her eggs in an egg-case with compartments: a separate room for each egg!

How did rats first come to western Europe?

They arrived by boat from Russia, slipping down the cables which tied the boats to the quays. The largest of them, **brown rats**, made their way to cellars and sewers where they lived and multiplied. In London there are as many rats as people! Brown rats live in groups and go out hunting for food at night, running along the edge of walls and squeaking in their shrill voices. They swim very well.

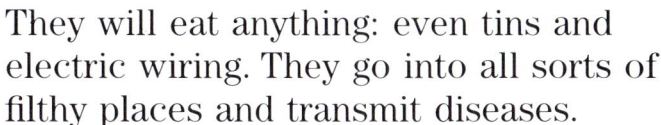

Rats are wonderful acrobats.

They will eat anything: even tins and electric wiring. They go into all sorts of filthy places and transmit diseases.

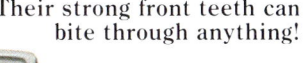

Their strong front teeth can bite through anything!

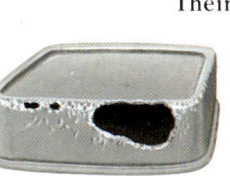

Bats can catch insects on the wing.

In attics, bats and barn owls sleep through the day.

They come out at night. The **barn owl** catches sparrows as they doze in the trees, or stays in for a supper of plump house mice...

Mice live everywhere among us. They make their nests under the floorboards or in a hole in the wall, lining them with bits of paper filched from our waste baskets. They may not eat much, but they eat anything, even soap and candles! They spoil a lot of food by nibbling at it.

Black rats live in attics too.

Up on high, the birds fly! House martins

use mud and twigs to build their nests, under the eaves of houses. They come back to the same nest every year.

Swifts arrive from Africa in April, and go back again in August. They spend all their time in the air! At night, they glide high up in the sky, instead of sleeping in a nest.

It never lands on the ground because it couldn't take off again.

Falcons are the fastest of all birds. In America, **kestrels** sometimes live at the top of skyscrapers. In Europe, kestrels live on rooftops and in church-towers.

Jackdaws caw from their roosts on the chimneypots.

Wood-pigeon and collared dove

Pigeons are the monarchs of the city centres.

They swagger along the pavements hardly bothering to get out of your way!

They build their nests on the ledges of tall buildings which remind them of the cliff-sides where their ancestors used to live. The female gathers together a few twigs, and lays a couple of eggs. She feeds her nestlings with a special liquid from her crop.

There are too many pigeons!

Their droppings foul our monuments and houses. They have to be caught in nets and sent back to the country.

Pigeons love bathing in puddles.

22

1. Chaffinch
2. Goldfinch
3. Great tit
4. Blue-tit
5. Robin
6. Stray cat
7. Blackbird
8. Magpie

In the parks and gardens,

the animals don't have such a cosy time!

The grass is mown, the plants are changed frequently, weeds are pulled out, trees cut back… All the same, these are the wild life reserves of the towns! You can hear birds singing there at dawn, marking out their territory. Can you recognise a **small tortoiseshell**? The wings of this pretty little butterfly (1) are bordered with blue. A **mole** (2) pokes its nose in the air. Every day, a mole will travel 30 metres of tunnels underground, chomping its way through the worms and snails it comes across. Acrobatic **squirrels** (3) can skim up trees faster than you can blink!

Hedgehogs (4) are noisy!
After nightfall, you can hear them snuffling, snorting and groaning round the garden as they search for seeds and insects to eat.

Hedgehogs love to eat **earthworms** (5). There are millions of worms under every lawn, filling the soil with air-holes which let the rain soak in.

This beautifully regular web is the work of the **garden spider** (6), who makes it from silk spun in its abdomen. Despite their fragile appearance the webs are very strong. You can recognise the garden spider by the cross on its back.

Up above the rivers and canals, gulls hover on wide white wings. These **black-headed gulls** glide along, calling out with their haunting, dipping cry, then settle on the water to drift with the current. Where do they go at night-time? They leave the towns and sleep in marshes nearby. They eat fish swimming just below the surface of the water, but they'll pick up food from dustbins and dumps as well! Their heads are white in winter and black in summer.

Mallard ducks, on their way to warmer countries, drop in. The males are brightly coloured with their green heads! Some fish, such as the **tench,** can live in quite stagnant water with very little oxygen.

1. Roach 2. Bleak 3. Gudgeon 4. Cat-fish 5. Tench

The male of the house cricket will spend hours singing to attract females by scraping its wings together.

What attracts ants?

Sugar. They'll often troop into a house, rank after rank of them, to feed on a few drops of honey or jam.

In gardens, they 'farm' greenfly, and milk them for the sweet liquid they produce. If you look carefully, you can see ants herding their flocks!

Ladybirds like greenfly too, but they like to eat them! Frightened ladybirds give off a fearful smell: then the birds don't want to eat them any more...

An ant on a leaf milking a greenfly

Don't be afraid of these big insects, they are totally harmless: they are craneflies.

A lot of butterflies spend the winter sheltering in houses or attics, their wings folded round them. Be careful not to disturb them.
In spring, they need to escape into the sunlight. But many of them wear themselves out, battering against the window-panes. Please open the window for them!

Small tortoiseshell

On hot days, you will see butterflies flying around the gardens. They suck up sweet liquid from the flowers. Their wings are covered in thousands of tiny, brightly-coloured scales, set out in all sorts of elaborate and beautiful patterns.

Peacock butterfly

In Florida, the swamps where the alligators used to live have been drained and built on. So the alligators have learned to live near man, and make their homes in the sewers.

Unexpected guests!
Alligators in New York, **wolves** in Moscow: all sorts of surprising animals live in towns! In India, you will find **sacred cows** wandering the streets. Bands of **macaque monkeys** flash by, appearing and disappearing as if by magic! They steal food from the gardens, but nobody chases them. In India, man and beast live peacefully together.

In Turkey, eagles nest among the minarets.

Because of the silver circles which appear when its wings are spread, this pretty bird is called a **dollar-bird**. In Asia, they spend their time perched on the branches of a tall pine, waiting for an insect to fly within reach.
In Japan, they nest on factory roofs.

The storks are back!
These are migrant birds which spend their winters in Africa, and return to Europe in the spring to build their nests.

A stork's nest on your roof is said to be a sign of good luck.

In winter, hunger makes foxes forget their usual caution, and creep closer to people's houses.

If you come across a bear, play dead!

That's the advice you'll get in the north of Canada: **polar bears** sometimes come into town in the autumn to fill themselves up if they haven't had enough to eat during the summer. They have to be tranquillised so that they can be caught and put back on the ice.

Do racoons have good table manners?

Yes! They wash their food before they eat it! They like living in the suburbs of American towns, rummaging in dustbins for food.

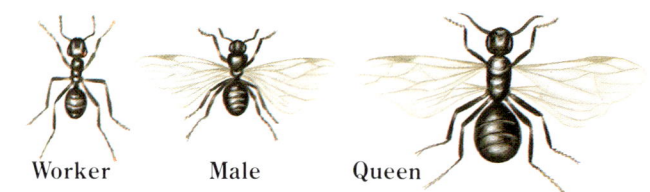

Worker   Male   Queen

What are all these flying ants you sometimes see in midsummer?

They are males and future queens. Once fertilised, each queen will find a hole to set up a new nest.

Barn owls leave their traces around town!

At the foot of trees or in attics, you may find the pellets which they bring up after eating a mouse or a little bird. The pellets contain the bones, feathers, skin: everything the owl can't digest! If you examine them, you can find out what the owl has been eating.

1. House martin
2. Swallow
3. Swift

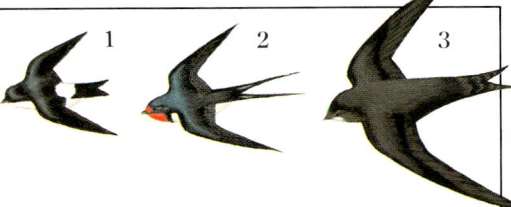

Learn how to recognise birds.

Observe the shape of their beaks and wings, and take note of their habits. Listen to their calls.
You will soon be able to recognise them easily.

Tracking animals

Learn how to recognise which animals have passed by...

Mouse

Rat

Feral cat
(domestic cat gone wild)

Fox

Index

alligators, 30
ants, 28,34
barn owls, 17,34
bats, 17
black rats, 17
blackbird, 23
bleak, 27
blue-tit, 9,23
brown rats, 15
butterflies, 24,29
cat, 23,35
cat-fish, 27
chaffinch, 23
cockroach, 13
cows, 30
craneflies, 29
crickets, 28
dollar-bird, 31
ducks, 27
eagles, 31
earthworms, 25
earwigs, 12
falcons, 18
fish, 27
fleas, 13
flies, 11
foxes, 32,35
garden spider, 25
goldfinch, 23
great tit, 23
greenfly, 28
gudgeon, 27
gulls, 27
harvestman, 10
head louse, 13
hedgehogs, 25
house martins, 18,35
house spider, 10
jackdaws, 18
kestrels, 18
lacewing, 9
ladybirds, 28
magpies, 23
mallard ducks, 27
mice, 7,17,35
mole, 24
monkeys, 30

mosquitoes, 11
moths, 7,12
pigeons, 7,21
polar bears, 32
racoons, 32
rats, 15,35
roach, 27
robin, 23
silverfish, 13
sparrows, 7
spider, 10
squirrels, 24
storks, 31
swallows, 35
swifts, 18,35
tench, 27
termites, 7,12
wasps, 9
wolves, 30
wood-worm, 12
woodlice, 13